ALL THINGS BUTTERFLIES FOR KIDS

FILLED WITH PLENTY OF FACTS, PHOTOS, AND
FUN TO LEARN ALL ABOUT BUTTERFLIES

ANIMAL READS

WWW.ANIMALREADS.COM

THIS BOOK
BELONGS TO...

_____

_____

CONTENTS

WELCOME TO THE ENCHANTING WORLD OF BUTTERFLIES

These colorful fluttery creatures enchant both young and old. They look so friendly as they hustle and bustle up and down on their way to their next flower.

Insects usually get a bit of a bad wrap. **Yucky creepy crawlies, right?!**

Would it surprise you that these colorful beauties are actually insects? Maybe not... but perhaps some of these crazy things will?

Did you know that butterflies taste with their feet? Or that some of these magical creatures can change color? Can you believe there are actually 17,500 different kinds of butterflies alive today, and they all play an important role in the well-being of the world? **It's all true!**

In the United States alone, there are 750 different species of butterflies.

17,500 is a big number, and it can be hard to picture exactly how many that is in real life. Here's a fun way to help.

Imagine you are a butterfly buff (*We bet that, like us, you are!*) Every day after school, you hunt for butterflies. But your goal isn't to find lots of the same kind of butterfly.

Your goal is to find lots of different species of butterflies. You are looking for *monarch butterflies*, *swallowtails*, and many others, which we will learn all about later in this book. Once you find a monarch butterfly and check it off your list, you aren't looking for any more of that kind.

Just how long do you think it will take before you can check off all 17,500 butterfly species on your list? If you found 10 different species each day, it would still take you **3 whole years to find all those kinds of butterflies!** That includes looking for butterflies 365 days a year—*even on Christmas,* *your birthday, and every other holiday.* **Pretty crazy, huh!**

There is so much to explore about butterflies, and we are about to go on a fluttery adventure to learn all about these insects. We'll meet some of the most interesting and amazing butterflies from all over the world and discover all about their unique lives. Are you ready to enter the world of these delicate, beautiful, and important creatures?

Alright then, let's go!

I'M GONNA
WING IT!

WHAT IS A BUTTERFLY?

Butterflies are insects and, like many other insects, they have 6 legs, an abdomen/body, a thorax, a head, wings, and 2 antennae that stick up from the top of their head.

Butterflies also have an **exoskeleton.** This means their skeletons are on the outside and help to protect their soft inner parts.

These fluttery insects are part of the *Lepidoptera* order and in the suborder *Rhopalocera*. These strange *names, orders*, and *suborders* can seem intimidating at first, but they are very helpful for scientists and researchers.

They help us learn more about animals and help categorize all the amazing creatures we find on our planet.

Depending on what group an animal is a part of, researchers can understand right away what unique features the animal might have. For example, they may have a certain body type, wings, perhaps 3 toes, or even different types of teeth or mouths.

Not surprisingly, butterflies are also closely related to moths, who are also a part of the *Lepidoptera* order.

WHAT LOOKS LIKE HALF A BUTTERFLY?

The other half!

CHARACTERISTICS AND APPEARANCE

Most of you probably think you know exactly what a butterfly looks like. Imagine you are learning about butterflies at school. Your teacher holds up a picture of a butterfly and asks you how many wings you see.

Oh, that's easy, right? **Obviously, a butterfly has two wings!**

Actually, that's not right at all. *Surprised?*

What most people don't realize is that a butterfly has **four** wings, not two. The reason for the confusion is because the two wings on each side overlap and are connected, so they appear to be almost one whole wing.

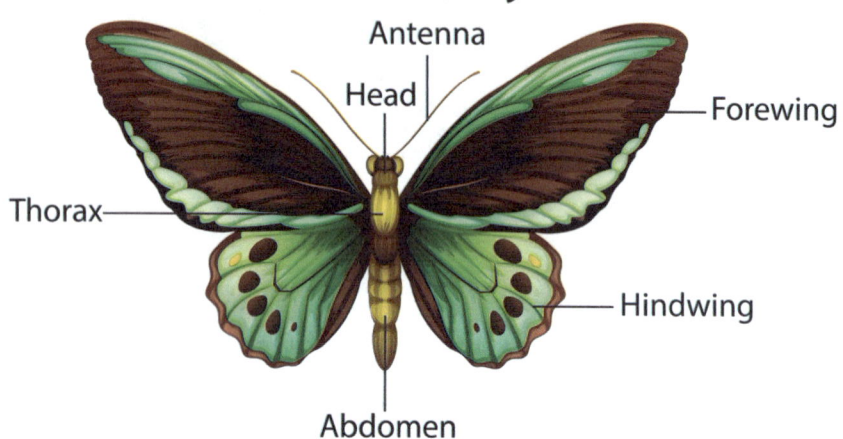

The forewing (*or top wing*) is what is used to power the butterflies flight. But don't let that make you think the hindwing (*bottom wing*) isn't important too! The hindwing allows the butterfly to fly much faster and also helps with its ability to turn in the air.

Butterfly wings are actually transparent or see-through. The decorative colors and patterns that appear on the wings are actually from the scales that cover the butterflies wings, body, and legs.

Now you may be thinking, *"Scales?! I've never seen a butterfly with scales!"*

As you learned earlier, butterflies and moths are part of the *Lepidoptera* group. All species in the Lepidoptera group have scales over their bodies and wings.

But unlike fish or dragons, these scales don't really look like scales at all. They are actually flattened hairs that create the different colors and patterns that butterflies are so well-known for.

The scales are another reason that you have to be very careful when handling a butterfly. It is very easy to damage a butterfly and brush off the scales by accident. It is best not to touch the wings at all and just let butterflies land on you.

Butterflies also have *compound eyes*, much like flies. This means that their eyes are made of thousands of tiny receptors that help them figure out colors and other things to help their vision. Butterflies have good eyesight and can even see colors like green, red, and yellow, which animals like our beloved dogs and cats can't!

Flowers have actually adapted to have the beautiful colors they do to attract pollinating insects like butterflies and bees.

WARM OR COLD?

Butterflies actually share something in common with snakes. *Do you know what it is?*

No, butterflies don't slither, and snakes don't fly (*thankfully*)!

Butterflies, like snakes and most reptiles, are **cold-blooded**. To be cold-blooded means that the temperature of the animal or insect isn't always warm.

Instead, the outside temperature around the butterfly determines how warm or cold they are. You are warm-blooded. That means unless you are sick or have a fever, your temperature inside your body is always 98.6 degrees, even if it is cold or hot outside. But a butterfly's temperature goes up or down depending on how hot or cold it is around them.

Outside temperature is very important to butterflies. Butterflies actually can't fly if they get too cold because ice crystals will form on their wings. And, last we checked, no one sells butterfly coats or wing warmers for our fluttery friends.

So, what do butterflies do in winter if they can't get too cold? Depending on the species, butterflies handle the problem of winter in one of two ways. Some butterflies **hibernate** all winter long until the warm weather returns. Like bears and several rodent species, butterflies go into a deep sleep that allows their body to slow down and survive the cold winter. Hibernating butterflies cluster together into holes, under leaves, in dead trees, in caves, and hang upside down by their *tarsi*, which are little claws on the ends of their feet. The tarsi enable the butterflies to clamp onto leaves or twigs.

Another way butterflies hibernate is they will stay in their ***larval stage***. This is a stage in a butterflies life when it is a caterpillar that will begin to wrap itself into a type of sleeping bag. It's such a unique process that we will learn about later in the book.

Butterfly species that don't hibernate have another answer to avoiding the cold of winter. These butterflies choose to **migrate** instead. Migration is a seasonal trip that an animal or insect takes to a new place. Migration usually occurs at the same time each year.

Monarch butterflies, a species you will learn more about soon, are some of the best-known migrators in the butterfly world. They can travel up to 2,000 miles to reach warmer climates in Mexico or California.

WHAT DO BUTTERFLIES EAT?

Do you know that you and butterflies probably share a few favorites when it comes to food? *No, it's not tree sap.* Although butterflies love the stuff, we're guessing you probably don't like a good tree sap sandwich. Nectar is another favorite for butterflies, but you probably don't care for that either.

What about fruit or fruit juice? Do you like orange juice with your breakfast, or do you cheer when watermelon season comes around again? Butterflies love fruit juice too, and they even love rotting fruit.

Since you have teeth, you can chew your food. But have you ever seen a butterfly with teeth? Probably not.

Butterflies don't have teeth, lips, or a mouth like yours. Instead, they have a **proboscis**. The proboscis is a tube-like straw that is the butterflies mouth. With it, the butterfly sucks up food like nectar or juice. This is one reason why butterflies only eat liquid food—they can't chew and can only suck up their food.

If you have ever had a butterfly land on your arm, do you know that it was actually *tasting* you? **It's true!** Butterflies have the strange but incredible ability to taste with their feet.

It seems a little weird. Imagine if that were true for you. Every sandy beach you walk on barefoot would be a little different, wouldn't it? **And just imagine what your socks must taste like!**

But for a butterfly, being able to taste with their feet actually comes in handy. Think about it. Butterflies land on plants, fruit, and flowers. The ability to taste and know if something is food or not right away is pretty helpful.

The receptors on a butterflies feet allow them to taste the surface they land on and decide whether it would make a good meal or not. They are also closely linked to smelling as well.

If a butterfly hasn't eaten you yet, we're guessing you thankfully aren't a delicious meal. But who knows!

PREDATORS AND DANGER

Butterflies, like most animals and insects, have **predators.** Predators are other animals or insects that survive by eating other species. Who is on the list of dangerous acquaintances for a butterfly? This list is actually pretty long! Wasps, flies, frogs, spiders, and even birds all love to find a tasty butterfly snack.

Have you ever seen a butterfly with hard armor like a shield bug? Or have you ever been stung by a butterfly? Probably not because they can't sting!

Thankfully, butterflies have adapted other ways to protect themselves from some of these natural enemies. Even if they don't look tough, butterflies are no easy prey.

What can butterflies do to protect themselves out in the world where predators lurk at every turn? Some species use camouflage to make it hard for predators to find them. There's a really cool species called the dead leaf butterfly that you will learn about a bit later. It has adapted to have wings that look like a dried-up leaf when its wings are folded. **No bird, frog, or insect wants to eat a dried-up leaf!**

Some species use their bright colors as a warning to predators to leave them alone. *How can a color be a warning?*

Bright colors in the natural world tend to signify danger or that something is toxic. Butterflies use their colors to tell predators to watch out, I just might be super unhealthy for you!

Some species have even adapted to use the toxins produced by the plants they eat and developed the ability to be toxic themselves. Predators learn that certain colors or designs mean they will feel sick if they eat that bug. The butterfly also might not taste very good.

The really cool thing is that many butterflies have adapted to look like toxic species, even when they don't have any toxins at all. This is called **mimicry**, and it means to *mimic* or act like another species.

It's kind of like putting on a karate suit and walking down the street when you don't know karate at all. Nobody would mess with you, right? They would figure you must know karate! Butterflies do this too, and mimic the colors or look of other "**tougher**" kinds of butterflies. Predators get confused and leave them alone too.

Have you ever watched a butterfly fluttering around? They don't usually fly very straight, do they? They bumble along in the area, going up and down, and flip around, eventually landing on a flower.

This unpredictable and bumbling flight pattern is also a means of defense. Some butterflies that don't have toxins or use mimicry fly in an unusual pattern like this because it makes them harder to catch. A bird watching from a tree can't swoop in and grab the butterfly if it doesn't know where it is going to go next!

Camouflage, toxins, mimicry, and unusual flight patterns are all ways butterflies stay safe to live another day in the **bug-eat-bug** world of nature.

WHERE DO BUTTERFLIES LIVE?

Did you know that butterflies live on every continent of the world except for Antarctica? It's true! Butterflies live in a wide variety of habitats, from forests to grasslands, mountains to rainforests, to even your backyard. Wherever there are the right plants for food, and it's not too cold, you can find butterflies.

However, more and more habitats for butterflies are disappearing as cities grow larger, and there are fewer wild spaces left.

The biggest cause for the extinction of butterflies is their disappearing habitat. Butterflies need plants to live. They need flowers to eat. They need green spaces and native plants that offer them everything they need. But in cities, especially crowded cities with little or no yards, butterflies have a hard time finding a place to call home.

Butterflies who migrate need a place to call home in two different places—*a winter home and a summer home*. The monarch butterfly for example, travels or migrates when the weather turns cold. They need places to live and food to eat when they reach their sunny vacation home in Mexico.

But in the last 20 years, monarch butterflies have been disappearing at a very concerning rate. There are 80% fewer monarch butterflies than there were just 20 years ago.

WHAT DO YOU SAY WHEN YOU THROW A PIECE OF BUTTER OUT OF THE WINDOW?

BUTTER-fly!

DIFFERENT SPECIES OF BUTTERFLIES

As you learned earlier, there are 17,500 different species of butterflies in the world today. If we made a butterfly book listing each species, it would turn out so big we don't think you'd be able to lift it!

So, we thought it would be better if we looked at some of the most common butterflies you will likely see fluttering by on a fresh spring day. After that, we will introduce you to a few super strange, interesting, and unique butterflies that you may not have heard about before.

COMMON BUTTERFLIES IN NORTH AMERICA

Monarch Butterfly (Danaus plexippus)–

Common in both North and South America, the monarch butterfly is one of the best-known species around. These butterflies are large with a 3-to-4-inch wingspan. They are very recogniz-able with their bright orange wings with a white-dotted outline.

Monarchs are one of the longest-living butter-flies. However, with a long life, the monarch butterfly has the problem of cold winters to deal with. Monarchs are known for their yearly **migration**, which means they take a long trip, sometimes up to 3,000 miles.

Each winter, they travel to warmer places such as Mexico or California. Amazingly, the monarch butterfly is the only species to migrate 2 ways. This means they go South for the winter, lay eggs, and then travel back North again. What is also incredible about these butterflies is that they can be spotted migrating together, creating what's called a **migratory wave**.

This type of wave has nothing to do with water, but the millions of butterflies moving together are like waves in the air. It is definitely a spectacular sight!

Monarchs also have a special way of protecting themselves against predators such as birds. As they grow, they eat certain leaves called milk-weed. These leaves are toxic for birds and other animals that eat butterflies, and monarchs can use these toxins for protection. If a bird eats a monarch, it gets sick to its stomach. Plenty of birds now know it's better not to eat these fluttery beings since they will get sick.

Spring Azure Butterfly
(Celastrina ladon) –

Imagine you've just come through a gray and dreary winter. *What is a sign, besides green buds on the trees, that signals Spring is here?* One sign is the arrival of the spring azure butterfly.

This butterfly is a welcome cheery friend and is one of the first butterflies people see in the Spring. These beautiful butterflies are tiny, as they only grow to be about 1 inch, and are bright blue. They often live on the edges of woods or cedar swamps, and they are also a frequent visitor to garden flowers.

These butterflies have some of the shortest lifespans of all butterflies. They tend to live less than a week long, with a typical lifespan of only 2-5 days. This is enough time to **pollinate** (*we will learn all about what this means a bit later in the book*) some plants and lay eggs.

Black Swallowtail Butterfly
(Papilio polyxenes) –

The Black Swallowtail Butterfly is a very common butterfly in backyards and gardens of North America. Especially more towards the Eastern two-thirds of the United States.

These elegant butterflies are mostly found in open areas, such as fields, meadows, parks, and open forests. Especially where there are plenty of flowers.

This elegant species is large and mostly black, with males typically having yellow dots and females having blue dots.

FEMALE & MALE

They are particularly attracted to parsley, dill, and carrots and will lay their eggs on these plants. If you plant these in your garden, chances are you will soon find some bright green and black caterpillars happily munching away.

These larger butterflies also typically have a lifespan of around 1 week. With such a short lifespan, this butterfly does not migrate and stays around its neighborhood.

Painted Lady Butterfly/
(Vanessa cardui) –

This gorgeous butterfly is one of the most common butterfly species on the planet. You can find this fluttery species on every continent except for Antarctica and South America.

They can be found in meadows, parks, forests, and gardens.

Like the Monarch Butterfly we learned about earlier, the Painted Lady here is also an avid traveler. This species also migrates long distances to survive harsher cold weather.

Scientists have discovered that this species can travel around 2,000 miles for their migration. *That's quite the trip, don't you say!*

They can flutter all the way from tropical Africa up to Northern Europe and back. This is a total distance of around 9,000 miles. *How do they get this done?* They do this in steps and in multiple generations. Isn't that special! These tiny creatures with brains the size of tiny dots can find their way across continents and back. To their credit, they can fly pretty quickly for butterflies reaching top speeds of 30 miles per hour.

The females of this impressive butterfly species can also lay about 500 eggs in their lifespan. That's a whole lot! We think the most famous egg layers are chickens... and they can lay around 250 eggs in an entire year. Painted lady butter-flies, on the other hand, lay their 500 eggs in less than a month!

Eastern Tiger Swallowtail/
(Papilio glaucus) –

These are definitely some elegant-looking butterflies. The Eastern Tiger Swallowtail is pretty
big for your average butterfly as they can grow to
be around 5.5 inches. Females are usually larger
than males in this species.

If you look closely, you will see that these beautiful butterflies have big black stripes running
down their wings... *kind of like those on a tiger*! The
males of this species are also always yellow,

which gives them even more of a tiger feel. The ladies, on the other hand, can be yellow or black with some blue coloration towards the lower ends of their wings.

Eastern Tiger Swallowtails can be found throughout most of the United States and Canada. There they can be seen fluttering through forests, orchards, gardens, parks, and by water streams.

What's truly interesting about this spectacular-looking species is that the males have a secret weapon to attract female partners. They can produce a special perfume-like odor through *pheromones*, which the female species love. It's like putting on a great-smelling cologne or perfume before going on a date, just in the butterfly world.

Common Buckeye Butterfly/
(Junonia coenia) –

This next butterfly species is definitely a looker. It's easy to recognize the Buckeye as they have bright and colorful spots on their wings that look like eyes. These eyes give this butterfly species an intimidating appearance, and they actually developed this unique look for protection.

When potential predators stumble past a buckeye, their unique pattern startles them. *Eyes like that can't be on a butterfly!* So rather than potentially mess with something bad, they move on.

Aside from their intimidating eye spots, the buckeye is mostly brown, with 2 orange bars on each wing. They can also have a splash of white or light beige on the edge of each wing.

Buckeyes can be found throughout the United States. Still, they are most typically present in the southern states and Mexico. They love fluttering around more open areas with plenty of flowers and sunny meadows.

They have an average size and can grow up to 2.8 inches. Buckeyes also don't have incredibly long lifespans, as they usually only live for 20 days.

AMAZINGLY UNUSUAL BUTTERFLIES

A butterfly bigger than a bird! A butterfly that looks like a dried-up leaf! Here are a few of the strangest and most unusual species, each with fascinating facts of their own.

Dead Leaf Butterfly (Kallima inachus) –

As incredible masters of disguise, the dead leaf butterfly looks exactly like its name! When this butterfly's wings are closed, the wings look like a dried-out brown leaf.

That may sound like a pretty ugly butterfly, but there is more than meets the eye with the dead leaf butterfly. When their wings are spread apart, bright orange and blue colors show this butterfly can still be stunning and exotic.

Dead leaf butterflies can be found in Southeast Asia, India, and Japan. They prefer a rainforest habitat where they can have their pick of rotten fruit that often lies on the forest floor. *If you are ever in those areas and find a dried-up brown leaf, look a little closer.* **It could be a butterfly!**

Zebra Longwing Butterfly
(Heliconius charithonia) –

The zebra longwing butterfly has a lot in common with its namesake, the stripey zebra. Found in Central America, Mexico, Texas, and Florida, this black butterfly is decorated with dramatic yellow or white stripes and, you guessed it, long, narrow wings that span an impressive 4 inches.

Zebra longwing butterflies are very graceful with a slower flight speed than some of the zippier species. They have been studied and shown to have a social order within their groups and appear to be very intelligent.

Zebra longwing butterflies were able to remember where food was and return back to the same location even when the food was taken away. This smart and unique butterfly also gets the distinction of being the state butterfly of Florida.

Birdwing Butterfly (Ornithoptera alexandrae) –

The birdwing butterfly, also called the *Queen Alexandra's birdwing butterfly*, lives a tropical life on the island of Papua New Guinea, which is a coastal island near Northern Australia. The female birdwing butterflies are not much to write home about, just a plain brown color with white stripes. But the males!

They are a beautiful blue and green color with a large black stripe on each wing. The wings of this species are very slender and long. These very rare and exotic butterflies have the honor of being the largest butterfly in the world!

With an impressive wingspan of 12 inches (1 foot), these butterflies also move their wings in a similar way to birds, which is why they have their name. Unfortunately, these butterflies are endangered because they only live in one region of the whole world and have suffered a decline because of deforestation of the rainforests.

They are also in decline because of collectors who remove the butterflies from their habitat, even though selling or buying birdwing butterflies is illegal.

Wow, that was quite the array of butterflies, right? Which was your favorite? For us, it's pretty hard to pick just one!

YOU

BUTTER

BELIEVE IT'S TRUE!

WHY HUMANS NEED BUTTERFLIES

Preserving butterflies isn't just about taking care of an insect that is beautiful and helps to add to the variety of nature. **Butterflies are also very important to our very existence!**

Butterflies, like bees, are pollinators. Pollinators are insects that collect pollen from one plant and spread it to another. Many plants cannot produce vegetables, fruit, or nuts without being pollinated. Think about it! A world without apples, peaches, squash, sugar, coffee, and pumpkins?

Unthinkable, right! And this is just the start of the list. Many parts of our food supply rely on pollinators like butterflies.

So, the next time you see a butterfly, thank it for the work it does to put food on our tables every day!

YOU COLOR THE WORLD!

A HISTORY OF BUTTERFLIES

Have you ever wondered where butterflies get their name? Scientists and historians are not really sure where the name came from, but it has been around for a long time. The Old English word for butterfly is *buttorfleoge*. There are a few stories about the name.

One tale is that long ago, farmers noticed butterflies hanging around their buckets of milk that were set out to be churned into butter. Since they thought the insects were attracted to the butter, they named them butterflies. This story isn't that far-fetched since butterflies do like sweet liquid.

Another idea is that many species of butterflies have yellow wings, which is the color of butter. Whatever the true history behind their name, it seems to fit these lovely fluttering insects.

Even though the name *butterfly* has only been around since the Middle Ages, butterflies themselves have been around for much, much longer!

Scientists agree that butterflies have lived on earth for about 55 million years since the Paleocene era. However, butterflies evolved from moths, and moths seem to date back much earlier to the Triassic-Jurassic period, about 200 million years ago.

Unfortunately, there are not as many fossil records of butterflies and moths as there are of other insects. This is probably because of a couple reasons.

One, areas around lakes and ponds create the best climate for fossils to occur, but butterflies are not very plentiful in these areas. Two, butterflies are very fragile, and their bodies quickly decompose, which doesn't leave time for a fossil to be created.

However, the scales of moths and butterflies have been found in fossils, and other examples of moths and butterflies have been preserved in amber. The oldest known fossil of a butterfly (*the skipper species*) was found in Denmark and is 55 million years old.

Unlike some animal and insect groups, butterflies don't appear to have changed in big ways since prehistoric times. However, prehistoric butterflies probably didn't fly as fast and may have had mouths more like a caterpillar.

Scientists believe that butterflies developed their straw-like mouths, the proboscis, sometime around the end of the Triassic period. One theory is that the butterflies needed their straw mouths to drink from tiny amounts of water that were around in this dry and hot period.

WHAT'S ONE THING THAT WILL ALWAYS GIVE YOU BUTTERFLIES?

Caterpillars!

THE LIFE CYCLE OF A BUTTERFLY

Can you imagine a cow starting its life as a completely different animal? What if a cow wasn't just a baby calf but started its life as a snake? Then, at a few days old, the *cow-snake* goes inside a hard covering, and its very cells change into a completely different animal. When ready, the hard covering splits apart, and out steps a cow. **That would be pretty crazy, right?!**

As crazy as it sounds, every butterfly undergoes this kind of change or *metamorphosis*.

Throughout its life, every butterfly goes through four distinct stages. These stages are:

1) The egg stage

2) The larva stage (*Caterpillar*)

3) The pupa stage

4) The adult stage

Let's learn about each part of a butterfly's life.

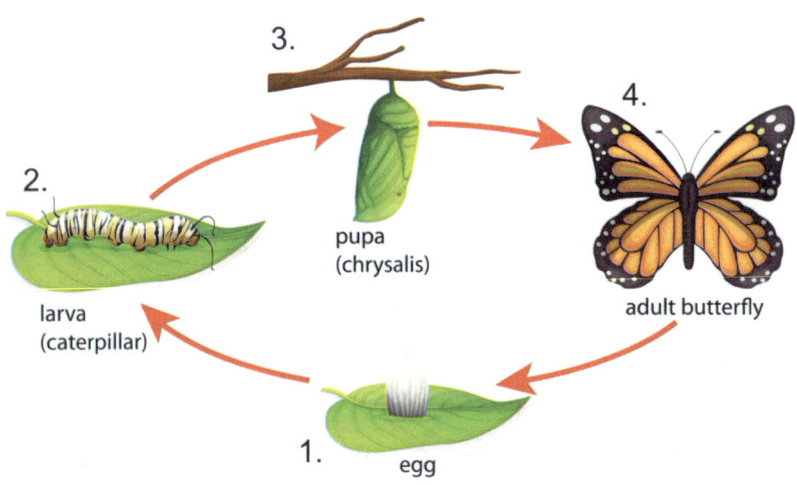

1. THE EGG STAGE

A female adult butterfly lays 1 to 300 tiny eggs, depending on the species. Each egg, which is only the size of a pinhead, holds a tiny caterpillar.

Most butterfly species only lay their eggs on a particular kind of plant or plant family. This is called the *host plant*. This plant will offer all the nutrients that the hatching caterpillars will need to survive.

The eggs are sticky and attach to the leaves of the host plant. Each egg will take 3-6 days to develop, and when ready, the caterpillars will hatch.

Unfortunately, life for an egg isn't easy. Many other insects love to eat a tasty butterfly egg. Only 1 out of every 100 eggs survives and hatches.

If the egg makes it to hatching, the next stage starts.

2. THE CATERPILLAR/LARVA STAGE

A caterpillar has one job in life—**to eat!** The newly-hatched caterpillar enjoys eating the leaves of the plant it was hatched onto. Caterpillars have **mandibles**, which are strong jaws, and they are great at chomping down food.

Some caterpillars are even considered pests to farmers because of the damage they can do to crops. Of course, one caterpillar can't cause too much trouble, but imagine a whole field of them!

Caterpillars only get about 5-10 days before they are ready to enter the next stage of development. As the caterpillar grows, it sheds its outer skin like a snake. It will do this about 4-5 times in this stage. By the end of this stage, the caterpillar will be about 2 inches long.

3. THE PUPA STAGE

When the caterpillar is nice and plump and fully grown, a hormone is released that tells the caterpillar to stop its endless eating. Its new job is to now find a place to stay for the next stage of its development.

The pupa will attach itself to a branch or underside of a leaf with a tiny bit of silk. Hanging upside down, the pupa will shed its skin. Most butterfly species don't form a cocoon, like moths do. Instead, the hard inner skin of the pupa protects it during this stage. *It is called a **chrysalis**.*

During the next 7-10 days, the pupa will undergo a remarkable change. This process is called **metamorphoses**, which is Latin for "*changing shape.*" During this time, the pupa will experience a total breakdown of almost every part of its body!

Enzymes called caspases dissolve the cells, muscles, and organs of the pupa. Inside the chrysalis is a big squishy mess. The only parts that don't liquify are the parts necessary to keep the pupa alive and breathing. Special cells that were formerly **dormant** or *asleep* now come alive. They hold the information necessary to turn the squishy mess in the chrysalis into a butterfly.

Some chrysalis become see-through in the last few days. If you are lucky, you might get a sneak peek into what is happening.

When the magical transformation is complete, the chrysalis splits open down the middle, and a butterfly emerges. A red liquid that is all the waste, poop, etc., from the time in the chrysalis also comes out.

4. THE ADULT STAGE

Our butterfly has now emerged from its chrysalis, and it is officially an adult! But this newly-born butterfly can't fly yet. A newly-emerged butterfly's wings need time to dry out and become less crinkled. After about 2 hours, the butterfly will be able to fly.

Depending on the species, an adult butterfly can live anywhere from 1 week to almost 1 year. The average butterfly only lives around 30 days. Monarch butterflies are one of the longest living species, and they live to be about 9 months old.

Now the adult butterfly's job is to eat nectar, pollinate plants, and look for a mate to reproduce and keep the life cycle going.

A butterfly's work is never done!

WHAT IS A PROBOSCIS?

Nobody nose!

MORE AWESOME FACTS ABOUT BUTTERFLIES

- Did you know that butterflies are pollinators, like bees? That's right! Without pollinators making sure plants have what they need to keep creating vegetables, fruits, and nuts, we would be in a pretty bad place. We rely on pollinators like butterflies to pollinate the plants that produce our food.

- Butterfly antennae are very important. The little knobs on the end of their antennae help the butterfly find food, find a mate, and find their way around!

- Want an easy way to tell a butterfly from a moth? Since not all butterflies are brightly colored, you can't always go off of appearance alone. Here is a neat trick. Only butterflies have knobs at the end of their antennae. So, if it has a bumpy knob, you know it's a butterfly.

- Did you know the fastest butterflies can fly up to 40 mph? That's pretty fast for an insect. However, most butterflies are not that fast and only fly around 5-12 mph.

LET YOUR DREAMS

TAKE FLIGHT!

HOW TO HELP BUTTERFLIES!

We hope you have enjoyed learning all about butterflies. These beautiful pollinators are very important to the natural world. If you would like to be a friend to butterflies, here are a couple easy things you can do:

1) **Plant a butterfly garden.** As you learned, butterflies don't lay eggs on just any old plant. Each species has a specific plant (or plant family) that it uses as a host plant to lay eggs on. The host plant offers the right food for that species' hatching caterpillars. If you would like to attract butterflies to your yard, look up what kinds of

butterflies are native to your area and what kinds of host plants they need. Before you know it, you'll have butterflies fluttering around all over the place! Plus, since lack of habitat is also a big reason for the decline in butterfly populations, you can feel good knowing you are helping out the pollinators who do so much for us.

2) Hand out some butterfly beverages. In the summer, put out a shallow water dish for butterflies to drink from or rest near. You can also partially fill it with sand and then keep it wet. Butterflies will come to drink the water and also love getting extra minerals from the sand as well.

3) Don't use pesticides! Pesticides have been shown to do a great deal of harm to pollinators like bees. Use natural weeding methods instead of chemicals.

Thank you for being a friend to butterflies! Together, we can enjoy our world and ensure that all species have a fair chance to thrive.

YOU MAKE US FLUTTER!

THANK YOU!

Thank you for reading this book and for allowing us to share our love for butterflies with you!

If you've enjoyed this book, please let us know by leaving a rating and a brief review wherever you made your purchase! This helps us spread the word to other readers!

Thank you for your time, and have an awesome day!

For more information, please visit:

www.animalreads.com

YOU'RE LOOKIN' FLY!

Published by Admore Publishing: Gotenstraße, Berlin, Germany

www.admorepublishing.com

Made in United States
Cleveland, OH
27 October 2025

24718599R00052